THE
TRIUMPH
OF LOVE

BOOKS BY GEOFFREY HILL

Poetry

For the Unfallen

King Log

Mercian Hymns

Tenebrae

The Mystery of the Charity of Charles Péguy

New and Collected Poems, 1952–1992

Canaan

The Triumph of Love

Prose

The Lords of Limit:
Essays on Literature and Ideas

The Enemy's Country: Words, Contexture,
and Other Circumstances of Language

Poetic Drama

Henrik Ibsen's 'Brand': A Version for the Stage

THE TRIUMPH OF LOVE

GEOFFREY HILL

Houghton Mifflin Company

BOSTON   NEW YORK

For information about permission to
reproduce selections from this book, write to
Permissions, Houghton Mifflin Company,
215 Park Avenue South,
New York, New York 10003.

Library of Congress Cataloging-in-Publication Data

Hill, Geoffrey.
  The triumph of love / Geoffrey Hill.
      p.   cm.
    ISBN 0-395-91235-0
    I. Title.
  PR6015.I4735T7   1998
  821'.914—DC21   98-19502   CIP

Book design by Anne Chalmers

Type: Monotype Perpetua

Printed in the United States of America

QUM 10 9 8 7 6 5 4 3 2

for

ALICE

and for

LUC

ואשלחה עליהם מלאכים לאמר מלאכה גדולה אני עשה ולא
אוכל לרדת למה תשבת המלאכה כאשר ארפה וירדתי אליכם:

MISI ERGO AD EOS NUNCIOS DICENS: OPUS GRANDE
EGO FACIO ET NON POSSUM DISCENDERE; CUR CES-
SARE OPORTET OPUS, SI DESISTERO ET DISCEN-
DERO AD VOS.

ICH ABER SANDTE BOTEN ZU YHN UND LIES YHN
SAGEN. ICH HAB EYN GROS GESCHEFFT AUSZU-
RICHTEN. ICH KAN NICHT HYNAB KOMEN. ES
MOCHT DAS WERCK NACH BLEYBEN · WO ICH DIE
HAND ABTHETT UND ZU EUCH HYNAB ZOGE.

AND I SENT MESSENGERS VNTO THEM, SAYING, I AM
DOING A GREAT WORKE, SO THAT I CAN NOT COME
DOWN: WHY SHOULD THE WORKE CEASE, WHILEST
I LEAVE IT, AND COME DOWNE TO YOU?

NEHEMIAH 6:3

THE
TRIUMPH
OF LOVE

I

Sun-blazed, over Romsley, a livid rain-scarp.

II

Guilts were incurred in that place, now I am convinced:
self-molestation of the child-soul, would that be it?

III

Petronius Arbiter, take us in charge;
carry us with you to the house of correction.
Angelus Silesius, guard us while we are there.

IV

Ever more protracted foreplay,
never ending — *o ewigkeit* — no act
the act of oblivion, the blown
aorta pelting out blood.

V

Obstinate old man — *senex*
sapiens, it is not. What is he saying;
why is he still so angry? He says, I cannot
forgive myself. We are immortal.
Where was I? Prick him.

VI

Between bay window and hedge the impenetrable holly
strikes up again taut wintry vibrations.
The hellebore is there still,
half-buried; the crocuses are surviving.
From the front room I might be able to see
the coal fire's image planted in a circle
of cut-back rose bushes. Nothing is changed
by the strength of this reflection.

VII

Romsley, of all places! — Spraddled ridge-
village sacred to the boy-martyr,
Kenelm, his mouth full of blood and toffee.
A stocky water tower built like the stump
of a super-dreadnought's foremast. It could have set

Coventry ablaze with pretend
broadsides, some years before that armoured
city suddenly went down, guns
firing, beneath the horizon; huge silent whumphs
of flame-shadow bronzing the nocturnal
cloud-base of her now legendary dust.

VIII

But how could there not be a difficult
confronting of systematics — the scale
of articulation notched up one grade at a time?
They have conceded me — I think, beyond question —
power of determination but without
force of edict.
If I were to grasp once, in emulation,
work of the absolute, origin-creating mind,
its *opus est,* conclusive
otherness, the veil
of certitude discovered as itself
that which is to be revealed,
I should hold for my own, my self-giving,
my retort upon Emerson's 'alienated majesty',
the *De Causa Dei* of Thomas Bradwardine.

3

IX

On chance occasions —
and others have observed this — you can see the wind,
as it moves, barely a separate thing,
the inner wall, the cell, of an hourglass, humming
vortices, bright particles in dissolution,
a roiling plug of sand picked up
as a small dancing funnel. It is how
the purest apprehension might appear
to take corporeal shape.

X

Last things first; the slow haul to forgive them:
Chamberlain's compliant vanity, his pawn ticket saved
from the antepenultimate ultimatum; their strict
pudency, but not to national honour; callous
discretion; their inwardness with things of the world;
their hearing as a profound music
the hollow lion-roar of the slammed vaults;
the decent burials at the eleventh hour:
their Authorized Version — it has seen better days —
'nation shall not lift up sword against nation'
or 'nation shall rise up against nation' (a later
much-revised draft of the treaty). In either case
a telling figure out of rhetoric,
epanalepsis, the same word first and last.

XI

Above Dunkirk, the sheared anvil-
head of the oil-smoke column, the wind
beginning to turn, turning on itself, spiralling,
shaped on its potter's wheel. But no fire-storm:
such phenomena were as yet unvisited
upon Judeo-Christian-Senecan Europe.
It is to *Daniel,* as to our own
tragic satire, that one returns
for mastery of the business; well-timed,
intermitted terror. How else recall
Mierendorff's ancient, instant, final cry —
madness — in Leipzig, out of the sevenfold
fiery furnace?

XII

Even the things that stood,
stood in unlikeness. The Hauptbahnhofsplatz,
only, had been bulldozed clear. There were some
particulars to be recalled; the wind
bore an unmistakable sour tang
of paper-rubble, close-packed ream on ream
scorched into flaking slab, slowly damped down,
fire- and water-ruin. He could not reconcile,
he said, either Pity or Terror with the justice
of their dereliction:

bacterial supernovae, half-life contaminants,
multi-cellular mischance, myriad-
tongued anomie, are as shadows, vapours to it;
creative nihilism, Götterdämmerung's toy
theatre (and here he cited Benn, Ernst Jünger).
Even with that Parisian oblation
of worked, reworked, burin-and-acid griming,
Rouault's then unknown, desolate
masterwork, the *Miserere,* even
there, he concluded, it seems we must be brought
hard up against the unlovely
body of Aesthetics.

XIII

Whose lives are hidden in God? Whose?
Who can now tell what was taken, or where,
or how, or whether it was received:
how ditched, divested, clamped, sifted, over-
laid, raked over, grassed over, spread around,
rotted down with leafmould, accepted
as civic concrete, reinforceable
base cinderblocks:
tipped into Danube, Rhine, Vistula, dredged up
with the Baltic and the Pontic sludge:
committed *in absentia* to solemn elevation,
Trauermusik, musique funèbre, funeral

6

music, for male and female
voices ringingly *a cappella,*
made for double string choirs, congregated brass,
choice performers on baroque trumpets hefting,
like glassblowers, inventions
of supreme order?

XIV

As to bad faith, Malebranche might argue
it rests with inattention. Stupidity
is not admissible. However, the status
of apprehension remains at issue.
Some qualities are best
left unrecognized. Needless to say,
unrecognized is not
unacknowledged. Unnamed is not nameless.

XV

Britannia's own narrow
miracle of survival
was gifted to us by cryptanalysts,
unpredictable Polish
virtuosi, it is now revealed,
grudgingly. One might have guessed.

Why, then, did Poland require
that last sacrifice of her cavalry
while she possessed such
instruments of cryptic-helio-
tropic strength, like the sunflower
that is both flamen
and lumen of her noble fields?
Flamen I draw darkly out of flame.
Lumen is a measure of light.
Lumens are not luminaries. A great
Polish luminary of our time is the obscure
Aleksander Wat.

XVI

Turing played well in defence.
Turing did not
play well in defence. Attack both
positions. Admit defeat.

XVII

If the gospel is heard, all else follows:
the scattering, the diaspora,
the shtetlach, ash pits, pits of indigo dye.
Penitence can be spoken of, it is said,

but is itself beyond words;
even broken speech presumes. Those Christian Jews
of the first Church, huddled sabbath-survivors,
keepers of the word; silent, inside twenty years,
doubly outcast: even so I would remember —
the scattering, the diaspora.
We do not know the saints.
His mercy is greater even than his wisdom.
If the gospel is heard, all else follows.
We shall rise again, clutching our wounds.

      XVIII

It is not [possibly a lacuna — ED]
whether we have the Psalms in Latin or Hebrew
nor by what authority such things are committed,
dismissed among the aeonic dense snowflurries:
it is not in the mortgaged conversions — the synagogues,
the cathedrals — to Caesar and the great Pharaoh.
Distinctions are as nothing, but identity
is pulled apart. Try definition — is this a dead
march or a death march? It is a dead march.

XIX

If you so wish to construe this, I shall say
only: the Jew is not beholden
to forgiveness, of pity. You will have to
go forward block by block, for pity's sake,
irresolute as granite. Now
move to the next section.

XX

From the *Book of Daniel,* am I correct?
Quite correct, sir. Permit me:
refocus that Jew — yes there,
that one. You see him burning,
dropping feet first, in a composed manner,
still in suspension,
from the housetop.
It will take him for ever
caught at this instant
of world-exposure.
In close-up he maintains appearance —
Semitic ur-Engel —
terminal agony none the less
interminable, the young
martyrs ageing in the fire —
thank you, Hauptmann — Schauspieler? —

Run it through again and for ever
he stretches his wings of flame
upon instruction.

XXI

What did I miss? — as the man said,
silence twanging over the sprung
trap. Soothsayers of Suetonius and the *Annals,*
touting fatal omniscience, what
actors they were! Steady
professionals, escapologists,
illuminati of smoke and stench,
to their blackened fingers' ends.
Should I leave it like this? Or should I add
that, for the life of me, I cannot
see my own future in prediction?

XXII

What *flagitia* ought to have meant
in good time to our senators, the Hebrews
pronounced upon daily in their estranged tongue.
They also, it is true, maintained
market-place charlatans and gross sibyls,
guilds of inclusive debasement.

But the solitary great ones — Isaiah, Amos,
Ezekiel — if only these could have been
translated into our statutes, if deified
Caesar alone were their agent of resurrection.

XXIII

What remains? You may well ask. Construction
or deconstruction? There is some poor
mimicry of choice, whether you build or destroy.
But the Psalms — they remain; and certain exultant
canzoni of repentance, secular oppugnancy. *Laus
et vituperatio,* the worst
remembered, least understood, of the modes.
Add political satire. Add the irrefutable
grammar of Abdiel's defiance.
And if not wisdom, then something
that approaches it nearly. And if not faith,
then something through which it is made possible
to give credence — if only to Isaiah's prophetically
suffering servant; if only by evidence
of the faithful women, Ruth and Naomi,
as they were, and as Rembrandt sees them,
the widowed generations, the irrevocable
covenant with Abraham which you
scarcely recall.

XXIV

Summon the leaders, the leaping captions,
numbers rolled from a drum: Cardanus
on the significance of eclipses,
Rathenau, 'industrialist and philosopher',
famous unnamed assassins' open tourers,
a road slicked in its dressing of lime pollen.
After some early clouds burn off
as predicted by the harbour master
we will have a clear day —
lake water chopping under paddle-boxes,
the scroll-wave motion of a carrousel,
jelly-green celluloid eye-shields; children
overexcited by rampageous clowns,
fire-breathers, artists of inept escape.

XXV

The hierarchies are here to be questioned. Lead on
Angelus Novus; show onetime experts presenting
aniline dyes as the intensest expressions
of coal-tar; let others develop 'man's
determinate action', for so Peirce dubbed it
in the wake of Chickamauga. Failing these,
bring others well-tried in the practical
worlds of illusion, builders of fabled masks,

their dancing clients
vanishing into the work
made up as lords and spiky blackamoors:
Unveil the dust-wrapped, post-war architects'
immediate prize-designs in balsa wood,
excelling fantasies, sparsely inhabited
by spaced-out, pinhead model citizens:
Florentine piazzas for Antarctica.
The augurs, finally: strangely possessed by doubt
whether to address the saturnine magistrates
concerning the asteroid, or the asteroid
on the nature of destiny and calculation.

XXVI

Grief — now, after sixty years — exacerbated
through its very absurdity; anger stalled again
for nations twice betrayed by our appeasements'
false equities of common ash; the moral
imagination an eccentric failure.
Laus et vituperatio, public, forensic,
yet with a vehement
private ambition for the people's
greater good — *Joannis
Miltoni, Angli, pro Populo Angli-
cano Defensio:* this and other tracts,
day-laboured-at, under great imposition:

as powers, far-radiant, inspiring
a broadly conceded European fame.
Laus et vituperatio, lost, rediscovered,
renewed on few occasions this century:
Guernica perhaps; or Prague itself,
the Charles Bridge with Hradčany, keeping watch,
in Kokoschka's sixty-year-old triple portrait,
beside Komensky and Tomáš Masaryk.

XXVII

One could hardly foresee the vintage hearse
exploding on impact. God — what a mess!
Instantaneous peristalsis: his eight
Brownings plus the gun-camera — all over
the evening editions — I'm not surprised:
Councillors of State exposed, 'their privy members
like unto those of horses'; nakedness
'unavoidable for duration?' Those
poor, ruined umbrellas.
This: *'ad Socium'*? A hefty
packet for All Souls, I shouldn't wonder.
Fresh intercepts too — the Bletchley magi! —
to the Master of St John's, 'for his advisement';
for the Provost of King's Coll:, less than nothing.
As to my Lord Protector: nothing
but name and number.

XXVIII

As I have at times imagined: Melancholy,
the more inert we are, thrusts us
into the way of things violently
uprooted. And there, for her own
increase, grants us a little possession,
that we may then lose all. *Boerenverdriet* —
peasant sorrow? peasant affliction? — you cannot
cease feeling their uncouth terror, whose flesh
is our own. The slaughterers relish this work
of sport: *landsknechts* as Callot depicts them,
hideously-festive-death's foragers;
so he draws them among us,
slouch-feathered, shin-booted, jangle
of sloven-worn iron: *ruyter, ritterkind,*
rutterkin, over the low shrub hill — hoyda!
hoyda! — heel-kicking their nags.

XXIX

What is this strange tree that bears so well
such heavy fruit commingled with new blossom;
and who are these
hanging amid the branches,
in bonds of remonstrance,
like traitors like martyrs?

This is our Upas tree; it is a tree of sleep
that never breaks; it is our politic
transcendent shade.
It is England's
iron-bound storm-tree turbulently at rest.

XXX

Bring out Behemoth — so; a sullen beast —
unentreated of the people. It has come
close to your name, with nominal disclaimer,
for your single glory, should that be spoken of,
your ignominy by nameless attribution.

XXXI

Scab-picking old scab: why should we be salted
with the scurf of his sores?

XXXII

Well-set imperial fixture — Victory's
equestrian stone cancan topping out
Constitution Arch. The city snarls,
the noon guns' heavy ripple shakes the dead.

What guns? Which dead? Haig, whom they justified
in his self-image to the tune of thousands?
The luckless stop-press vacancies? The regiments
rehiring by the week,
hoisting the dead-beat with galvanic
blatter of trumpets?

XXXIII

Trumpets? Come off it — that was cavalry!
Wavering bugles took the Chums and Pals.

XXXIV

Boom-boom! Obnoxious chthonic old fart,
boom-boom, boom-boom! No thanks to that stiff
Korzeniowski. Obsolete, shallow-draught,
fifteen-inch gun, ex-imperial
monitor, perched
rudderless on a mudbank in mid-river,
exposing himself to Borrioboola-Gha.

XXXV

Even now, I tell myself, there is a language
to which I might speak and which

would rightly hear me;
responding with eloquence; in its turn,
negotiating sense without insult
given or injury taken.
Familiar to those who already know it
elsewhere as justice,
it is met also in the form of silence.

XXXVI

You can say you are deaf in several languages —
lass es in Ruhe, mon vieux, hic scriptum est.

XXXVII

Shameless old man, bent on committing
more public nuisance. Incontinent
fury wetting the air. Impotently
bereft satire. Charged with erudition,
put up by the defence to be
his own accuser.

XXXVIII

Widely established yet with particular
local intensities, the snow

half-thawed now hardens over again,
glassen-ridged, or pashed
like fish-ice: refracted light
red against copper. The hedged sun
draws into itself for its self-quenching.
If one is so minded, these modalities
stoop to re-enter the subterrane of faith —
faith, that is, in real Being;
the real being God or, more comprehensively, Christ —
as a sanctuary lamp treadles its low flame
or as the long-exiled *Salve Regina* was sung
in the crypt at Lastingham on the threshold
of a millennium.

XXXIX

Rancorous, narcissistic old sod — what
makes him go on? We thought, hoped rather,
he might be dead. Too bad. So how
much more does he have of injury time?

XL

For wordly, read worldly; for in equity, inequity;
for religious read religiose; for distinction
detestation. Take accessible to mean

acceptable, accommodating, openly servile.
Is that right, Missis, or is that right? I don't
care what I say, do I?

XLI

For iconic priesthood, read worldly pique and ambition.
Change insightfully caring to pruriently intrusive.
Delete chastened and humbled. Insert humiliated.
Interpret slain in the spirit as browbeaten to exhaustion.
For hardness of heart read costly dislike of cant.

XLII

Excuse me — excuse me — I did not
say the pain is lifting. I said the pain is in
the lifting. No — please — forget it.

XLIII

This is quite dreadful — he's become obsessed.
There you go, there you go — narrow it down to *obsession!*

XLIV

Cry pax. Not that anything is forgiven;
not that there seems anything new to forgive
in this assemblance. Not that the assemblance
might be tempted into the fertile
wilderness of unspirituality. Not that I
know the way out, or in. So be it;
let us continue to abuse one another
with the kiss of peace.

XLV

It is believed — argued — they offered him
some kind of painkiller, which
is plausible. In any event
he would not touch it.
Morus, humble and witty at the end,
glad of a clean death;
Southwell, addressing the cordial
cordially: 'it does my heart good'.
Fifty years without limbs, or in an iron
lung, is that possible? I lose
courage but courage is not lost.

Not always. Not even. Hand me that *Latin*
Through Pictures. A thing
given is not always, or even, a gift,
Deodatus, sing *dona nobis*.
A gift is a donation. Donors are permitted
to give of themselves, with saints and martyrs,
kneeling at the altarpiece's edge,
catechumens of final judgement.
Unversed in our data, the secular
conjuring of insurances,
amid droughts, floods, plagues,
how delicate in self-exaction
they appear; with what severity
of graciousness in these and in like matters
they keep their places.
How carnally nonetheless
such things of the spirit are wrought by attrition;
what misplaced, mistimed,
hammering perfects them: the ephemeral
attacking the absolute
with ruining and/or ruined force.

XLVII

Movie-vocals cracked, her patter still
bright as the basement gents' brass taps at the Town Hall.
Benevolent, like a Young Fabians' Club
vision of labour; invariable routine
produced the same hot water, brought to the boil
her honest yodelling. So she fetched home the lads
from France, as once she had marched the lasses back
to a silent mill. She, and her armed
aspidistra, last off the beaches.

XLVIII

Sir, your 'Arts/Life' column claims that Gracie
Fields sang at Dunkirk. Is this
a misprint? For sang read sank? [Phew,
what a 'prang'! — ED]

XLIX

A clear half-face of the moon
at mid-day, above the cupola's intricately
graceful wind-vane's confected silver.
Everything sharp, bright. Memory in its recesses
pierced directly — *Lucifer*
ante portas. Why that?

L

Trimalchio, bouncing up from a brief seventh
bout of financial ruin, pledges us
his high-spent poverty with distasteful feast.
He is himself already, so he claims,
in his seventh element.
He merits, I would say, a loaded rumour
among the legends that now circulate
about Canary Wharf, the Isle of Dogs,
new comets whiffling in and out of orbit.
Time's satire, for its part, allows his status
not worse than that clay-footed emperor —
barely saluted at his last ascension — flung
arse-over-tip to belching Tartarus,
with coarsest imputations, by the gods:
roof-crashing his own dull funeral-orgy,
the never-finished ritual deification,
making a clown-shaped hole in the sacred floor.
Trimalchio readjusts his mask of laughter.

LI

Whatever may be meant by *moral landscape,*
it is for me increasingly a terrain
seen in cross-section: igneous, sedimentary,
conglomerate, metamorphic rock-
strata, in which particular grace,
individual love, decency, endurance,
are traceable across the faults.

LII

Admittedly at times this moral landscape
to my exasperated ear emits
archaic burrings like a small, high-fenced
electricity sub-station of uncertain age
in a field corner where the flies
gather and old horses shake their sides.

LIII

But leave it now, leave it; as you left
a washed-out day at Stourport or the Lickey,
improvised rainhats mulch for papier-mâché,
and the chips floating.
Leave it now, leave it; give it over

to that all-gathering general English light,
in which each separate bead
of drizzle at its own thorn-tip stands
as revelation.

LIV

Entertainment overkill: that amplifier
acts as the brain of the putsch. The old
elixir-salesmen had no such entourage
though their product was superior; as was
their cunning oratory.
For the essentials of the cadre, Wordsworth's
'savage torpor' can hardly be bettered
or his prescience refuted.
What it is they possess — and, at some mean
level, Europe lies naked to their abuse —
is not immediately
in the grasp of their hand. They are vassal-
lord-puppet-strutters, not great scourges of God.
A simple text would strike them
dumb, and is awaited. Meanwhile
they are undeniable powers of this world,
closely attended in their performance
of sacral baseness, like kings at stool.

Vergine bella — it is here that I require
a canzone of some substance. There are sound
precedents for this, of a plain eloquence
which would be perfect. But —
ought one to say, I am required; or, it is
required of me; or, it is requisite that I should
make such an offering, bring in such a tribute?
And is this real obligation or actual
pressure of expectancy? One cannot purchase
the goodwill of your arduously simple faith
as one would acquire a tobacconist's cum paper shop
or a small convenience store
established by aloof, hardworking Muslims.
Nor is language, now, what it once was
even in — wait a tick — nineteen hundred and forty-
five of the common era, when your blast-scarred face
appeared staring, seemingly in disbelief,
shocked beyond recollection, unable to recognize
the mighty and the tender salutations
that slowly, with innumerable false starts, the ages
had put together for your glory
in words and in the harmonies of stone.
But you have long known and endured all things
since you first suffered the Incarnation:
endless the extortions, endless the dragging
in of your name. *Vergine bella,* as you

are well aware, I here follow
Petrarch, who was your follower,
a sinner devoted to your service.
I ask that you acknowledge the work
as being contributive to your high praise,
even if no-one else shall be reconciled
to a final understanding of it in that light.

LVI

Less cryptic but still with a touch
of the enigmatic? Very well: how did
the ladies ride? What were they not wearing?
Who put their scent-mark on him
like a cat spraying? For what amour
did he wear a woman's wig? Who tried
to set fire to it?
Relate the *mystique* of Catchem's End,
Worcestershire, to the *politique*
of incomprehensible verse-sequences.
Is he or is he not posing *dévoué*
outside the Boutique des Cahiers
in the rue de la Sorbonne? —
his face is turned from the militant display
towards some other vision.
How would you define his body-language?
Stoic consensuality? Sceptic paranoia?

What was meant by 'the greatness
of the flame'? Who cried from the midst of it
'if this is *kenosis,* I want out'?

LVII

My dear and awkward love, we may not need
to burn the furniture; though, like you,
I understand by this time all too well
despair at the kiln-door — the first moment's
ultimate ruin of the final prize.

LVIII

Portrait of mourning's autodidact: proud,
not willing to drop the increasingly
evident burden of shamed
gratitude: to his own dead,
and to those not his own — Pandora
Barraclough, for instance;
his desire to keep alive
recollection of what they were put to, though
not for his sake, not for this future, and not
'rooted', God help us; they were as he
now is; dispossessed
even in the scant subsistence

of disturbed folk-memory. Each time,
the salving of the waste
less and less expected;
yet time and again salvific —
like the barely recognized
beauty of the potato vine in its places
of lowly flowering.

LIX

By *unearned grandiloquence* is to be understood:
congées not given, *pourboires,* backhanders,
neither passed nor winked at in passing.
But — yes — wounded pride is clownish, deadly.
I have a mind to recast this
as mere entertainment-interludes: crowned
Ignorance time-honoured; and Justice running
widdershins with a dagger of lath.

LX

Return of *Angelus Novus.* How that
must have shaken you — the anima
touched like a snare-drum
or the middle ear.
New conjugations, fine as hair-springs,

the seconds-hand twitching it-
self into shock.
Try it again — again you leap
aside and are riven.

LXI

A se stesso.
Not unworded. Enworded.
But in the extremity
of coherence. You will be taken up.
A se stesso.

LXII

A happy investment, Lord Trimalchio:
forasmuch as Blake laboured
in Hercules Buildings, and as 'up Dryden's
alley' is where he was set upon
to the unstinting plaudits of the trade;
as 'mob' and 'fun' came in at the same time:
forasmuch as the world stands,
in a small part, exposed for what it is —
tyrant-entertainment, master of the crowds.

LXIII

Those obscenities which — as you say — you fancy
perverting the consecration; you hear them all right
even if they are unspoken, as most are. It is
difficult always to catch the tacit
echoes of self-resonance. Is prayer
residual in imprecation? Only
as we equivocate. When I examine
my soul's heart's blood I find it the blood
of bulls and goats.
Things unspoken as spoken give us away.
What else can I now sell myself, filched
from Lenten *Hebrews*?

LXIV

Delete: sell myself; filched from. Inert:
tell myself; fetched from. For inert read insect.

LXV

Who posed as Britannia — one of royalty's
rare vestals, was it? Across the years so much
has been taken, too much given away —
more like evidence let
slip than as alms bestowed or restitution

arrived at. What we arrived at without fail,
national débâcle, was sometimes called victory.
India did for us finally, hideous
sub-continental death-rites, the widowed Queen-
Empress felled like Lenin, melted down; new
sacred monsters bellowing at the pyre.

LXVI

Christ has risen yet again to their
ritual supplication. It seems weird
that the comedy never self-destructs.
Actually it is strengthened — if
attenuation is strength. (Donne
said as much of gold. Come back,
Donne, I forgive you; and lovely Herbert.)
But what strange guild is this
that practises daily
synchronized genuflection and takes pride
in hazing my Jewish wife? If Christ
be not risen, Christians are petty
temple-schismatics, justly
cast out of the law. Worse things
have befallen Israel. But since he is
risen, he is risen even for these
high-handed underlings of self-
worship: who, as by obedience,
proclaim him risen indeed.

LXVII

Instruct me further in your travail,
blind interpreter. Suppose I cannot
unearth what it was they buried: research
is not anamnesis. Nor is this a primer
of innocence exactly. Did the centurion
see nothing irregular before the abnormal
light seared his eyeballs? Why do I
take as my gift a wounded and wounding
introspection? The rule is clear enough: last
alleluias *forte,* followed by indifferent
coffee and fellowship.

LXVIII

Remove my heart of stone. Replace
my heart of stone. Inspire
cardio-vascular prophylaxis. Stir
psychotic iconoclasts — Jan
van Leyden's crew — to a fresh blood-feast.
Shall I cease to abide by the tables
of Mosaic law, the intractable
midrashim of the rabbi who died
slowly by torture? Must I make my peace
with Clausewitz; or with Hobbes's law, the timid
aggressor, the stoner of providence?

LXIX

What choice do you have? These are false questions.
Fear is your absolute, yet in each feature
infinitely variable, Manichean beyond dispute,
for you alone, the skeletal maple, a loose wire
tapping the wind.

LXX

Active virtue: that which shall contain
its own passion in the public weal —
do you follow? — or can you at least
take the drift of the thing? The struggle
for a noble vernacular: this
did not end with Petrarch. But where is it?
Where has it got us? Does it stop, in our case,
with Dryden, or, perhaps,
Milton's political sonnets? — the cherished stock
hacked into ransom and ruin; the voices
of distinction, far back, indistinct.
Still, I'm convinced that shaping,
voicing, are types of civic action. Or, slightly
to refashion this, that Wordsworth's two
Prefaces stand with his great tract
on the Convention of Cintra, witnessing
to the praesidium in the sacred name

of things betrayed. *Intrinsic value*
I am somewhat less sure of. It seems
implicate with active virtue but I cannot
say how, precisely. Partaking of both
fact and recognition, it must be, therefore,
in effect, at once agent and predicate:
imponderables brought home
to the brute mass and detail of the world;
there, by some, to be pondered.

LXXI

If slab faces can be wolfish this appears
in the tall glare of sodium light on snow.
Fairground-mirror distortion kneads us all
stocking-masks. I have not forgotten
crowd-demonry, the pulley-grins of the Flemish
tormentors. Should I subpoena Callot's
and Goya's witness to that which is in
[read: of] the natural archetype? It is the sheer
descent, the acceleration, that for us
now is terrible: unselfbeing — each held
distracted in the doomed body-cockpit
by a velocity which is also inertia,
round-the-clock idle talk-down to impact.

LXXII

Ethics at the far edge: give the old
bugger a shove / gentleman a shout.

LXXIII

I may be gone some time. *Hallelujah!*
Confession and recantation in fridge.

LXXIV

For Cinna the Poet, see under *errata*.

LXXV

Corner to corner, the careful
fabric of our lives ripped through
by the steel claws of contingency. We are made
to make ourselves instruments
of violence and cunning. There seems no
hook on which we are not caught
except, by lot, those of the thorns and nails.
Vergine bella, now I am half-way
and lost — need I say — in this maze of my own
devising. I would go back and start

again; or not start at all, which might
be wiser. No. Delete the last four words.
Talking to oneself is in fact
a colloquy with occasion — *eppur*
si muove — or so I tell myself.
Extraordinary how *N*. and *N*. contrive
to run their depilators off the great turbine —
the raw voltage could flay them. Such
intimate buzzing and smooth toiletry,
mingled with a few squeals, may yet
draw blood from bloodless Stockholm. *Mea culpa,*
I am too much moved by hate —
pardon, ma'am? — add greed, self-pity, sick
scrupulosity, frequent fetal regression, *and*
a twisted libido? Oh yes — much
better out than in. *Morosa*
delectatio was his expression, that Irish
professor of rhetoric — forget his name.
Forget my own name next *in hac*
lacrimarum valle. But, to continue —

LXXVI

At seven, even, I knew the much-vaunted
Battle was a dud. First it was a dud,
then a gallant write-off. Honour the young men
whose eager fate was to steer that droopy *coque*
against the Meuse bridgeheads. The Fairey

Swordfish had an ungainly frail strength,
cranking in at sea level, wheels whacked
by Channel spindrift. Ingratitude
still gets to me, the unfairness
and waste of survival; a nation
with so many memorials but no memory.

LXXVII

By what right did Keyes, or my cousin's
Lancaster, or the trapped below-decks watch
of Peter's clangorous old destroyer-escort,
serve to enfranchise these strange children
pitiless in their ignorance and contempt?
I know places where grief has stood mute-
howling for half a century, self
grafted to unself till it is something like
these now-familiar alien hatreds,
coarse efflorescence over the dead
proprieties; strong words of Christian hope,
sub rosa, the unmentionable graffiti.

LXXVIII

You say how you are struck by the unnatural
brightness of marigolds; and is this manic,

or what. Are clowns depressives? The open
secret is to act well. Can the now silent
witnesses be questioned? What hope remains
to get him out alive? I'm sorry, her.
Tomorrow he died, became war-dead, picked
off the sky's face. Fifty years back, the dead
will hear and be broken. Get off the line.
Who are you to say I sound funny.

LXXIX

Time for a quick one, Petronius. Charged
with a violation of overnight
sumptuary laws, Custodian
of the Eyes, do not tempt further
the wrath of Priapus. Lie back. Enjoy.
Enjoy. Open another vein.

LXXX

Hopelessly-lost storyteller found.
Self-styled czar of ultimate
disaster movies says
everything must go. *Daniel*
a closed book.

LXXXI

Everyone on heat; *N.* and *N.* stinking,
unsated. Exposure to be at your ripest
discretion, Petronius Arbiter.

LXXXII

Go back to Romsley, pick up the pieces, becomes
a somewhat unhappy figure. I speak
deliberately like an old man who last saw it —
Romsley — through a spinning bike-wheel, as indeed
Kenelm may have done. That hook of ridge,
Waseley to Walton, was enemy country. Now
I overrun it in fiction. But Fairfield repels
my imperium, and always did. Its complex
anarchy of laws would have defeated Athelstan,
let alone Ine. High swine-pasture it was,
long before Domesday; and will be again,
albeit briefly, at the flash of Judgement.
Let it now take for good a bad part of my
childself. I gather I was a real swine.

LXXXIII

To have lost dignity is not the same
as to be humble. Is it so unjust
to say to the State Church you lack pride
and are not ashamed? But I have checked
pride with *Cruden:* fifty citations, three
in the new covenant, and not once
does it stand for a good will. I should call
Daniel proud but not high-minded, worthy
of all admiration. And Ruth, of her
lineage. Is Abdiel proud? Or the unknown
singer of Deborah? What am I to do
with these shards of downright majesty, this
ever-doubtful certitude, our curse,
our blessing, impacted as Hebrew?

LXXXIV

When you lift up your eyes and behold
afar off — look at it this way, not much
is expected of most AND (to have one's own
expectations) something of what they are ⎮leaps
to be recognized — when you lift up
your eyes and behold afar off: how
amazing it still is, the awaited name
hailed through our streets, under the pale leafage,

43

springing from the hierarchies of splendour
and salutation, prodigious messengers
with their own heralds and outriders —
yes, look! the Kenyan runners, look, there they go!
stippled with silver, shaking off the light
garlands of sweat —

LXXXV

A centrally-placed small round window, closed
under a pediment, caught and stared back my fear
centuries before I opened *The Franchise*
Affair. I am not unusually
sensitive to atmosphere, but one or two
fiery dreams of houses held
mid-day séance through my seventh year.
Photo-negatives I now accept
as the originals of this peculiar dread:
black façades, gap-windowed with solid-
glare flame, and with stark
figures caught in some unhuman
intimate torment I could not grasp
until I came to stills of the burning ghetto.

LXXXVI

Well over half-way now; still no response
from Angelus Silesius. These are harsh times
with hag Faith going the rounds. It is good
to be tempted and not fall. I remember
the Telgte synod: Grass in the chair,
vehemently imperturbable. A. S.
stayed for my paper. Was that Grass's suggestion?
Our theme was timely: '*Kinesis* to *Kenosis*'. Hold on —
that was the year after. 'Recidivism
of the *Deutschtum*'? Wrocław? No, Gdańsk. Hah —
'Guilt and Redemption in the *Trauerspiel*'!

LXXXVII

Forgive me, *Vergine bella,* if I return
to splenetics; they are not seemly,
a threat to both health
and salvation. A girl I once needed
to be in love with died recently, *Vergine
bella,* aged sixty-three. Forgive all such
lapses in time, and mend our attention
if it is not too late. Bless,
of your charity, for your orator's sake,
worthless *N.* and *N.* now Swedish millionaires.

LXXXVIII

Let him alone, let him
have his way, let him be touched
by his own angel, it will come to nothing:
born again, but stillborn.

LXXXIX

Stunned words of victory less memorable
than those urged from defeat; not that the vanquished
are more to be believed. In effect
it cries out for silence: whose
silence, would you say? I say endure
by way of enduring: the secular
masques, *Laus et vituperatio*. What
is ƎↃͶA⅃UꓭMA you may ask; has it come
down to us from the dead language of Canaan?

XC

Ur? Yes? Pardon? Miss a throe. Go to gaol.

XCI

Celebrate yet again the mind's eye's
dreadful kink or reach of resurrection —
the British walking-wounded — these are like
bunched final stragglers in a three-legged
marathon — last-gasp survivors, loud roll-calls
of the mute orphans, child-victims
in mill and mine. Here's your Lost Empire
Medal for a life spent giving blood. Not
celebrate. Calibrate. Seniors
to synchronize watches. Last rum and fireworks.

XCII

No way, Jane Grey, uncrowned bright
humanist: Boethius, Tully; Seneca, 'the old
moral man'; no way. The common
elm — *ulmus procera* — also gone
under, with the shires; though deer
are cared for, and the rare white cattle; as
is memory in this tranche of frozen sunlight.

XCIII

One thing then another, eh, sour
old Gower? Even in Latin your satire
well understands itself not well-disposed.
But in contempt — *Geffe juvat,* star-shards
rattling the coulter — and without leave,
under protest, with formal complaint, by
chance right of reply, the people —

XCIV

Suddenly they are upon us, the long
columns, the immense details
of betrayal: as always predicted
yet wholly unforeseen.
Incidents at the frontier — it is not
courage that is now in question.

XCV

This is not Duino. I have found no sign
that you are visited by any angel
of suffering creation. Violent
sensitivity is not vision, nor is vision
itself order. You may be possessed

of neurasthenic intelligence as others
have been tormented by helpless self-
knowledge, though I doubt it. In any event
I would not parade comparisons. Naked
experience as you preen it is a mild
indecency, like old-style London revue.
Indecent in turn, let me here interpose
the body of a parenthesis (do we indeed
not know ourselves?). You can always
say *I call you,* forcing my superior
hand at rhetoric. My question is
rhetorical, in that I expect
no answer. Would it be fairer to say
that I do not invite one? Let me allow
this to be no defence, merely a registration
of shock; and that, of course, I am putting
words in your mouth. Even so, I propose to
stay with this, perhaps to carry some meaning
of our imperfection.

XCVI

Ignorant, assured, there comes to us a voice —
unchallengeable — of the foundations,
distinct authority devoted
to indistinction. With what proximity
to justice stands the record of mischance,

heroic hit-or-miss, the air
so full of flak and tracer, legend says,
you pray to live unnoticed. Mr Ives
took Emersonian self-reliance the whole
way on that. Melville, half-immolated,
rebuilt the pyre. Holst, some time later,
stumbled on *dharma*. What can I say? —
At worst and best a blind ennoblement,
flood-water, hunched, shouldering at the weir,
the hatred that is in the nature of love.

XCVII

Devouring our names they possess and destroy
by numbers: the numbered, the numberless
as graphs of totality pose annihilation.
Each sensate corpse, in its fatal
mass-solitariness, excites
multiples of infliction. A particular
dull yard on a dull, smoky day. This, and this,
the unique face, indistinguishable, this, these,
choked in a cess-pit of leaking Sheol.

XCVIII

You will have seen how a big humming-top
walks its ferrule on a few inches of floor,

as if rehearsing the Torah. You see also
how this man's creepy, though not creeping, wit —
he fancies himself a token Jew by marriage,
a Jew by token marriage — has buzzed, droned,
round a half-dozen topics (fewer, surely?)
for almost fifty years: travestying
The Testament of Beauty. Denial
seems the *mot juste*. What did he say? He said,
I think, 'for Ashkenazic read Sephardic'.

XCIX

So be that jaw- and rib-stove
gabardine hump of pain
sopping the cobble-slime with its rag beard.
Don't even pray. Don't give them any more
to work on — I can understand that. If
witness meant witness, all could be martyrs.

C

Blitzkrieg crazes the map-face. Europa wakes
abruptly multi-fissured, the demiurge
rewriting things in her dust. *Mit welchem Recht?* —
Freud's outburst, strange as it seems, though he
meant being lied to. Courage is exposed
to the crack of nerves and pétards. *I*

don't wish to know that, I don't wish to know
that! Here's a better suggestion: have
black-out for six years and find her again
irreparably repaired.

CI

Though already too late we must
set out early, taking the cinder
path by the old scythe-works. There will be
no quarrel between us — all this time —
a light rain unceasing, the moist woods
full of wild garlic.

CII

You are right, of course; I neither stand
my ground nor run. In whatever direction
kinesis takes me, it is no distance.
In part like Blake's carnalists — *they
became what they beheld* — I am seen
to work my daysman's stint in the foul mill.
One could say that Hobbes (of Malmesbury), whom I
would call the last great
projector of Europe prior to Hudson
[Hudson the Railway King — E D], is radical
as we are *déracinés;* granted that *Leviathan*

towers on basics rather than from roots;
and that *roots* itself, unhappily, is now
a gnostic sign among the Corinthians.

CIII

Parades of strength are not, in the long view,
Aristotle's magnitudes. Langgasse,
in Danzig, sparked a short fuse. The massed
hakenkreuz-banners appeared as machine-fresh
robust street-hangings, crests of the phalanx,
terror's new standards. I do not recall which
death-camp it was that sheltered Goethe's oak
inside the perimeter. I cannot
tell you who told me or in what footnote
it sat hidden. This and other *disjecta*
membra, the abused here drawn
together with pain for their further dis-
memberment, I offer to the presiding
judge of our art, self-pleasured *Ironia.*

CIV

Self-pleasured, as retching on a voided
stomach pleasures self. Savage indignations
plighted with self-disgust become one flesh.
Pasternak, for example: *shestdesyat*

shestoy, they shout — give us the sixty-
sixth [sonnet, of Shakespeare — ED]. You could say
that to yourself in the darkness before sleep
and perhaps be reconciled. Nothing true
is easy — is that true? Or, how true is it?
It must be worth something, some sacrifice. I
write for the dead; *N., N.,* for the living
dead. No joke, though, self-defenestration.

CV

Mea culpa, mea culpa, Geffe juvat.
Take out supposition. Insert suppository.
For definitely the right era, read: deaf in the right ear.

CVI

You: with your regular morning and evening
glossolalia timed like the angelus;
your high mass choreographed by smoke-
sacristy ephebes — *choreograph* is the word
revealed to them; who are you to protest?
You: with the mantra sewn into your alb,
your rigidity and your abandonment,
your proud ignorance of doctrine, contempt
for the protracted, indeterminate,

passion-through-history of the English Church,
the Church of Wesley, Newman, and George Bell.

CVII

Flos campi–time again among the small
ruins, vestiges, memorials, of the uprooted
midlands railways. How suggestive the odour
of hawthorn, building from the rubble
of craft and graft. What was it that growing
girls could get from *Virol*? Were boys forbidden it
for their green-sickness? Could it have fed
our mutually immature desires? How
English, how vivid, how inapposite
to the disnatured century: a slow, Lydian-mode
wayfaring theme for unaccompanied viola.

CVIII
— Well as I hear I hear you but as I
hear you you are in dumb-show. —

Oculos tuos ad nos converte: convert
your eyes, *Vergine bella:* you gave us
a bit of a turn there. Not unnaturally —
but not naturally, either — they conceived
light to be the prime agent,
or mover, of generation. And as that
light embraced you, so you embraced
this conception; became — secured
by the eternal — its mortal source
and tenure: though many, perhaps most,
would argue against the relevance
of the Scholastics. What do you mean,
what have they to do with it, and have I
studied *The Sceptical Chymist?* Salt, sulphur,
mercury: more potent by far
than metaphysics whose demoted angels
have been caught dancing
with impropriety. Who's Impropriety? *Mea
culpa,* ma'am, a nervous tort.
Since when has our ultimate reprobation
turned (*oculos tuos ad nos con-
verte*) on the conversion or
reconversion of brain chemicals —
the taking up of serotonin? I
must confess to receiving the latest
elements, *Vergine bella,* as a signal
mystery, mercy, of these latter days.

No matter that the grace is so belated;
no matter who staked out and reaps
the patent-commodity; no matter how
grace is confused, repeatedly, with chill
euphoria. *Ad te suspiramus,*
gementes, flentes: which, being interpreted,
commits and commends us to loving
desperately, yet not with despair, not
even in desperation.

CX

This glowering carnival, kermesse of wrath
and resentment, how early — ? Very. Very deep
among elementary mayhem: *Seventy Years*
a Showman, A Book of Golden Deeds, The Worst
Journey in the World: Finders. Keepers:
Dandy, Beano, Film Fun, Radio Fun, mis-
teachers of survival: Laurel and Hardy
cutting, pacing, repacing, their
flawless shambles: J. A. in Scripture class,
under the desk lid, perilous comic strips
of dentures blown from trumpets: swift
economy of outline evidenced
by aircraft recognition cards: six days
a week — Saturdays off — the sustained,
inattentive, absorbing of King James' English.

But is such anger genuine or factitious,
Mr Editor? inquires a sincere
correspondent of the *Pink 'Un*. To which
that proper rag, adding only the word [*sic*],
makes answer rhadamanthine: Patriot Blood
is a great horse, so is Eurovista,
Kristallnacht is at stud. The odds
are against High Prophecy. Heap
ashes on your head and split your sides.
Since you have asked, however, we can say
the donkey Nehemiah has been lamed
but not withdrawn. Noble Vernacular
must be one of the fancies, as must Savage
Indignation, Pity, Boerenverdriet.
Lothian [MacSikker — E D] told us he saw
a draft typescript: caulk on caulk
of liquid eraser, illegible, overwrought,
more like psoriasis or scabies than
genuine inspiration. Séan O'Shem
said — trenchantly — that the man's epigraphs
are his audience; he needs to be heard;
they are his faction; only for them he's not
factitious. Or did you perhaps intend
fictitious? It's self-evident he can't
keep up a fiction, even for twenty lines.

CXII

The glowering carnival, kermesse of wrath,
caravans of the hermaphrodite
children of Plato, their genius
'strangely neglected': a man in an iron cage
lifted from Bunyan; the magic
lantern found among Empson's effects —
'works like a dream, lacking some slides of Hell' —
rare *tableaux morts-vivants,* the gift
of Ruysch-Leopardi; a mindless
cogitation and final
exhaustion of the automata;
the once-unequalled broken to advance
the unequal captains; general apocalyptic
uninventiveness on all sides: rumour
of Jewish alchemy, Rathenau
cold in his furs.

CXIII

Boerenverdriet? You eat it — it's Dutch liverwurst.

CXIV

From the Angels of Irrational
Decision and of Reversed Order

to the Angel of Improvisation:
from the Angel of Improvisation
to the Angels of Tannic
Acid, Salicyl, and Plain Water:
from the Angel of Advantage — where is
the Angel of Recorded Delivery? —
from the Angels of Advantage
Lost, of Sacrifice, of Surrender,
to the Angels of Merciful
Intervention and Final Custody.

CXV

Overburdened with levity, the spirit found
in carnal disarray — so what do you know,
Amarilli, mia bella? Say it is not
true that mockery is self-debasement;
though already I have your answer: We
are to keep faith, even with self-pity,
with faith's ingenuity, self-rectifying cadence,
perfectly imperfected: e.g., the lyric
art of Spanish baroque, seventeenth–
eighteenth-century Italian song,
which so aspires to make adamant *I*
am melting, the erotic, thrilled and chaste.
(End with that reference, in the Ludlow masque,
to *haemony,* plant of exilic virtue.)

What a fool! And what folly! I should have stuck
to Lucian from the start. Erasmus, More
[*Morus* — E D], how could it fail, that lineage?
As before, the question stands as one
of rhetoric. Wealth — *copia* — was required
to buy moderation: Lucianic
or Erasmian moderation, that is. *Morus*
enacted extreme measures, though not
overmuch — now and then a Lutheran
zealot *in flagrante*. And though the line did
fail, it was not from that cause nor
for any reason. Memory
and attention died, *comme ça,*
which is not reasonable. Polity regroups
and is guarded, where on D-Day men
drowned by the gross, in surf-dreck, still harnessed
to their lethal impedimenta.
Moderation can wring Jonah for comedy —
see Lucian, *supra,* and other analogues —
Despondency will bend iron, and *Much-afraid*
was a strong man's daughter — he said,
setting aside his stalled ode for thirty
vicarious rounds of bare-knuckle.

CXVII

A noble vernacular? We could screw him,
finish him, for all that. Then he ought
to be happy: a reborn ageing child,
privileged to no place of honour, sated
with dissatisfactions; his wardrobe
of curial cast-offs,
student of Livy in his father's house,
his father being the bailiff — three pounds
a week, rent-free. But all that *unheimlich*
work of his: salutes and cenotaphs,
and vessels moving seaward, the ebb tide
purled in their wake. We cannot
have some great instauration occurring
by default, can we?

CXVIII

By default, as it so happens, here we have
good and bad angels caught burning
themselves characteristic antiphons;
and here the true and the false
shepherds discovered
already deep into their hollow debate.
Is that all? No, add spinners of fine
calumny, confectioners of sugared

malice; add those who find sincerity
in heartless weeping. Add the pained,
painful clowns, brinksmen of perdition.
Sidney: best realizer and arguer
of music, that 'divine
striker upon the senses', steady my
music to your Augustinian grace-notes,
with your high craft of fret. I am glad
to have learned how it goes
with you and with Italianate-
Hebraic Milton: your voices pitched exactly —
somewhere — between *Laus Deo* and defiance.

CXIX

And yes — bugger you, MacSikker et al., — I do
mourn and resent your desolation of learning:
Scientia that enabled, if it did not secure,
forms of understanding, far from despicable,
and furthest now, as they are most despised.
By understanding I understand diligence
and attention, appropriately understood
as actuated self-knowledge, a daily acknowledgement
of what is owed the dead.

CXX

As with the Gospels, which it is allowed to resemble,
in *Measure for Measure* moral uplift
is not the issue. Scrupulosity, diffidence,
shrill spirituality, conviction, free expression,
come off as poorly as deceit or lust.
The ethical *motiv* is — so we may hazard —
opportunism, redemptive and redeemed;
case-hardened on case-law, casuistry's
own redemption; the general temper
a caustic equity.

CXXI

So what is faith if it is not
inescapable endurance? Unrevisited, the ferns
are breast-high, head-high, the days
lustrous, with their hinterlands of thunder.
Light is this instant, far-seeing
into itself, its own
signature on things that recognize
salvation. I
am an old man, a child, the horizon
is Traherne's country.

CXXII

Sitting up, I drift
in and out of sleep. It now appears
too much is owed, impossible to repay:
Memoria, the loan-shark.

CXXIII

The secular masque, advanced
by computation, has not otherwise
progressed. Millennial authority
makes necromantic the fire-targeted
century. African new-old
holocaust suffers up against
the all-time Hebrew *shoah*. But shaking
with aeonial palsy the screens
have failed Tomorrow and the victory
altars of the sacrificed engineers.

CXXIV

The glowering carnival, kermesse of wrath —
the pressure's beginning to tell now, you
can hear it, the creaking bounce
of the Miltonics: *But to my task ... But*

to my task, I ask you! He also cribs
from Dryden and *Vox Clamantis*. Recently
it's got much worse; like a provincial
actor-manager. What's more — when Arno
blundered at Firenze and the bronze
Baptistry doors bulged like tarpaulins, when
the flesh of the frescoes knew corruption —
he wasn't there, as Croker pointed out.

CXXV

I have been working towards this for some time,
Vergine bella. I am not too far from the end
[of the sequence — E D]. It may indeed be my last
occasion for approaching you in modes
of rhetoric to which I have addressed myself
throughout the course of this discourse. Custom
is strange — as I believe, ma'am, you well know —
not least in its familiar
power of estrangement. Estrangement itself
is strange, though less so than the metaphysics
of tautology, which is at once *vain
repetition* and *the logic of the world*
[Wittgenstein]. Some of its moves — I mean
tautology's — call to mind chess-moves: moves
that are in being before you — even as
you — make them. An actual play-through

from the Last Quartets could prove superfluous,
except to a deaf auditor. Then there is this
Augustinian-Pascalian thing about seeking
that which is already found. Tautology,
for Wittgenstein, manifests the condition
of unconditional truth. Mysticism is not
affects but grammar. There is nothing
mysterious in grammar; it constitutes
its own mystery, its *practicum*. Though certain
neologisms — Coleridge's 'tautegorical'
for example — clown out along the edge,
τὸ αὐτό enjoys its essential being
in theology as in logic. The intellectual
beauty of Bradwardine's thesis rests
in what it springs from: the Creator's grace
praecedentem tempore et natura ['Strewth!!!
'already present in time as in nature'? — ED]
and in what it returns to — our arrival
at a necessary salvation. So much
for the good news. The bad is its correlate —
everlasting torments of the non-elect; guaranteed
damnation for dead children unbaptized.
Wyclif and Dame Julian would have raised
few objections or none to those symmetries.
The Church's first martyrs, the Holy Innocents,
unbaptized Jewish infants, surrogates
of the Jewish child we call our Child-King —
small impediments that Policy deals with,

takes care of: *baptized in blood.* But surely
every new-born child is baptized in blood.
Still, there they are: crying shame to the cant,
the unending *negotium,*
the expediencies, enforcements, and rigged evidence.
Vergine bella, forgive us the cunning
and the reactive, over-righteous
indignation, the self-approving
obtuse wisdom after the event,
our aesthetics and our crude arrangements.
I have been working up to this. The Scholastics
mean more to me than the New Science. All
things are eternally present in time and nature.

CXXVI

To the short-sighted Citizen
Angel, the Angel of Assimilation —
'I will not run, dance, kow-tow, to entertain
thugs, perverts, parvenus, perjurers' —
from the stifled Lamentation Angel.
To that dying power from the trim,
well-clad Angel of Death: his insignia
and instruments————————
From that, to the violated Angel
of Eternal Audit. And to eternity
the ashen-fleshed, wrenched-silent,
untouched, unhearing, Angel of Forgiveness.

68

CXXVII

In loco parentis — devoured
by mad dad. Hideous — hideous — and many like it —

CXXVIII

The rough-edged, increasingly concave,
line of advance
stops dead: machine-guns do the work
of trick photography. The next trick also
requires apparatus: a sector
chitters brave tries at synchronized push-ups;
by magic the order stands — to remain — pitched
slightly forward against unseen resistance.
Cocteau *flânéed* the First War. After the Second
he moved angles, elevations, to revitalize
young gay men mercurial whom he lifted
out of the tribunals, fabled interrogations,
the cellars, of his fantastical *milice*.
Dipping their (rubber-sheathed) hands to the wrist
in vats of quicksilver, they were absorbed
by bedroom-mirrors through which the interchange
of life with death began and ended. It
is hard now to recover how his debellated,
debellished land bore to inaugurate
towers of remembrance, the massive
verticals, to lean on fields of the dead;

the fields of preservation, with ranging
shadows cast by the black bulk
of light, that are formal sorrow, mourning,
in its conjurations of triumphs.

CXXIX

One or two illustrations might help us —
Geffe — to take a fix on your position,
anomalous as it is. Two Kokoschkas
and one Rembrandt: Rembrandt's unfinished
The Concord of the State, OK? The Masaryk
portrait and *What We Are Fighting For,* OK. OK?
ta-Rah ta-Rah ta-rarara Rah

CXXX

Milton — the political pamphlets. Blake
in old age reaffirming the hierarchies.
Péguy *passim,* virtually. Bernanos,
if only for having written *la colère
des imbéciles remplit le monde.* Radnóti
at Bór. The great self-recovery of Wat.
ta-Rah ta-Rah ta-rarara Rah

CXXXI

Mourning registers as celebration. Haydn
at sixty-six, his clowning majesty
of invention never bettered [he means,
I think, the late 'Erdődy' Quartets — E D].
Bartók dying in New York, unfinished
music among the sickbed detritus:
ta-Rah   ta-Rah   ta-rarara   Rah

CXXXII

I would have liked to know — I may yet know —
whether the hidden part which most engages me
is closer to nub, crux, crank, or orifice.
Crank, probably. The system which converts
rotary to rectilinear motion is called
the eccentric. Whichever it is, it has my tie.
ta-Rah   ta-Rah   ta-rarara   Rah

CXXXIII

The nerve required to keep standing, pedaling,
grinning inanely, strikes me (*splat!*) as more
than temperamental luck. It is a formal
self-distancing, but like choreography.

You could clog to some late Haydn without
injuring either tradition. Please — my *foot* —
ta-Rah   ta-Rah   ta-rarara   Rah

CXXXIV

It surprises me not at all that your
private, marginal, uncommitted writing —
this is to be in code — came at the end
to the forum of world acclaim. *Decenza* —
your term — I leave unchallenged; decorum
aloof from conformity; not a mask
of power's harsh suavities. [Internal
evidence identifies the late
Eugenio Montale as the undoubted
subject of this address. — ED] It sets you
high among the virtuous *avvocati* —
the judges with a grasp of such vocation —
and puts you with the place-brokers, purveyors
of counsel, publishers, editors,
and senators-for-life; a civic conscience
attested by comedy: twenty-five years
with the *Nuovo Corriere della Sera*
as leader-writer and critic of first nights;
still your own man; publicities, public life,
the anteroom to the presence-chamber
of self-containment. (Machiavelli described

entering his study, robed as if for Court.)
But one man's privacy is another's
crowded *at home* — we are that circumscribed.
Machado who, to say the least, is your
grand equal, sat out his solitude, habitué
of small, shaky, wicker or zinc tables —
still-life with bottle, glass, scrawled school-*cahiers* —
put his own voice to slow-drawn induration.
I admire you and have trained my ear
to your muted discords. This rage twists
me, for no reason other than the sight
of anarchy coming to irregular order
with laurels; now with wreaths: Duomo drone-
bell, parade-mask shout, beautifully-caught
scatter of pigeons in brusque upward tumble,
wingbeats held by a blink.

CXXXV

So what about the dark wood, eh?
When do we come to the dark wood? —
We have already been sent to the dark
wood, by misdirection: Trônes, Montauban,
High Wood, Delville, Mametz. We have been there,
and are there still, in a manner of speaking.

73

CXXXVI

But only in a manner of speaking.
I was not there, nor were you. We are children
of the Thirties, the sour dissipation;
England at once too weepy and too cold.

CXXXVII

The glowering carnival: nightly solar-flare
from the Black Country; minatory beacons
of ironstone, sulphur. Then, greying, east-northeast,
Lawrence's wasted pit-villages rising early,
spinning-wheel gear-iron girding above each
iron garth; old stanchions wet with field-dew.

CXXXVIII

Confound you, Croker — you and your righteous
censure! I have admitted, many times,
my absence from the Salient, from the coal-face
in Combs Pit, Thornhill. Yes, to my shame,
I high-tailed it at Pozières (Butterworth
died in my place). At Arras I sacrificed
Edward Thomas (the chief cause of your
hostility — why can't you say so?). I find

your certitudes offensive. My cowardice
is not contested. I am saying (simply)
what is to become of memory? Yes — I know —
I've asked that before.

CXXXIX

Concerning the elective will, *arbitrium*.
Concerning wilfulness and determination:
in so far as the elective is elect
it will not now be chosen. It may choose
non-election, as things stand. The Florentine
academies conjoined
grammar and the Fall, made a case of *casus*.
All things by that argument are bound
to the nature of disordinance (*eat
shit, MacSikker*). Judgement is forever
divided, in two minds, over the broken
span of consequence: *richly deserved:* how can
our witty sorrows try the frame of such
unsecured security — nothing between
election and reprobation, except vertigo
and a household word-game of tit-for-tat
with family values. Milton writes of those
who 'comming to Curse . . . have stumbled into
a kind of Blessing'; but if you suppose him
to invoke a stirrup-and-ground-type mercy, think

again. It's a Plutarchan twist: even our foes
further us, though against their will and purpose (*up
yours, O'Shem*). Hopkins gave his two best
coinings of the self — *inscape,*
instress — to Lucifer for his self-love,
non serviam: sweetness of absolute
hatred, which shall embrace self-hatred,
encompass self-extinction, annihilation's
demonic angelism. Hereditary
depression is something else again. You
can draw up Plutarch against yourself; yourself
the enemy (*do it and be damned*). Hopkins
had things so nearly right, as did Herbert,
though neither would have flown solo (the Angel
of the Agony was in attendance).
As for the rest of us, must we describe
Finnegans Wake as a dead end? (*Over
my dead body,* says Slow.)

CXL

A se stesso: of Self, the lost cause to end all
lost causes; and which you are not (are you?)
so hopeless as to hope to defend. You've
what? Leopardi for the New Age? Mirageous
laterite highway — every few miles
a clump of vultures, the vile spread.

Fama/Fame [It. — ED]: celebrity and hunger
gorging on road-kill. *A se stesso.*

CXLI

From the terrible Angel of Procreation
to the Angel-in-hiding of Senility.
To the Autonomous Angel
from the several Angels of Solitude:
cc Angel of Self-Alienation,
Angel of Solitary Confinement.
From the Angel of the Morning Gold-fix
to the Angels of Mandragora and Rip-off.
To the Demotic Angels from the Angels
of Repulsion-Attraction, the loud-
winged Angels of Equal Sacrifice, the sole
Angel standing in for Hope and Despair.

CXLII

To the Angel of the Approved Estimates,
to the Angels of Promise Across the Entire
Spectrum. To the Surplus Angels of Acquisition.
I cannot even hear the new instructions,
let alone obey them. Where,
you will say, does explanation

end and confession begin? To know all
is to forgive all: a maxim more wicked,
even, than it is stupid — forgive me,
would you, ever? — But that, by my reckoning,
is not the sum. I have introduced,
it is true, *Laus et vituperatio*
as a formality; still this formal thing
is less clear *in situ*. That —
possibly — is why I appeal to it. The Angels
of Sacral Equivocation, they now tell me,
are redundant: we have lost the *Bloody Question*
[*vide* State Trials (Elizabethan) — ED].
Though you can count on there being some
bloody question or other, one does more
than barely survive. Less hangs on the outcome,
or by, or around, it. Why do I think —
urgently — of beach-sewage? At one source,
Moltke, the two Bonhoeffers, von Haeften,
suffered the Bloody Question and did
nobly thereby. Late praise costs nothing.
To the Angels of Inconclusive Right
on Both Sides, to the Angel of the Last
Minutes, to the Angel of Our
Estimated Times of Arrival and Departure.

CXLIII

Power and sycophancy, sycophancy in power:
power's own cringing to extrapolation
and false prophecy. Subways of white tile
smeared with obscene brown banners. Foucault
running there for his life. Synaesthesia
of appeasement's brain-stench.

CXLIV

Now, for the Law, the Prophets, must we take
inspired guesswork; for inspired guesswork, inter-
locked ignorance, vanity, fear, hope?
It's a difficult line — I can just hear
Unwisdom grinding like fury, the farthest
breaking of Nations. Even beyond that,
distorted sound-patterns of grace. Is this
Manichean? No — Manichean! What?
Lauda? Lauda? Lauda Sion? LAUDA!

CXLV

Incantation or incontinence — the lyric cry?
Believe me, he's not
told you the half of it. (*All who are able may stand.*)

The whole-keeping of Augustine's City of God
is our witness; vindicated — even to us —
in a widow's portion of the Law's
majesty of surrender. A hundred
words — or fewer — engrafted by Tyndale's
unshowy diligence: it is all there
but we are not all there, read that how you will.
Cursed be he that removeth his neighbour's mark:
Mosaic statute, to which Ruskin was steadfast.
(If Pound had stood so, he might not have foundered.)
Paul's reinscription of the Kenotic Hymn —
God . . . made himself of no reputation . . . took
the shape of a servant — is our manumission,
Zion new-centred at the circumference
of the world's concentration. Ruskin's wedded
incapacity, for which he has been scourged
many times with derision, does not
render his vision blind or his suffering
impotent. Fellow-labouring master-
servant of *Fors Clavigera,* to us he appears
some half-fabulous field-ditcher who prised
up, from a stone-wedged hedge-root, the lost
amazing crown.

CXLVII

To go so far with the elaborately-
vested Angel of Naked Truth:
and where are we, finally? Don't
say that — we are nowhere
finally. And nowhere are you —
nowhere are you — any more — more
cryptic than a schoolyard truce. Cry
Kings, Cross, or Crosses, cry Pax,
cry Pax, but to be healed. But to be
healed, and die!

CXLVIII

Obnoxious means, far back within itself,
easily wounded. But vulnerable, proud
anger is, I find, a related self
of covetousness. I came late
to seeing that. Actually, I had to be
shown it. What I saw was rough, and still
pains me. Perhaps it should pain me more.
Pride is our crux: be angry, but not proud
where that means vainglorious. Take Leopardi's
words or — to be accurate — BV's English
cast of them: when he found Tasso's poor
scratch of a memorial barely showing

among the cold slabs of defunct pomp. It
seemed *a sad and angry consolation*.
So — Croker, MacSikker, O'Shem — I ask you:
what are poems for? They are to console us
with their own gift, which is like perfect pitch.
Let us commit that to our dust. What
ought a poem to be? Answer, *a sad*
and angry consolation. What is
the poem? What figures? Say,
a sad and angry consolation. That's
beautiful. Once more? *A sad and angry*
consolation.

CXLIX

Obstinate old man — *senex*
sapiens, it is not. Is he still
writing? What is he writing now? He
has just written: I find it hard
to forgive myself. We are immortal. Where
was I? —

CL

Sun-blazed, over Romsley, the livid rain-scarp.

ABOUT THE AUTHOR

Geoffrey Hill was born in Bromsgrove, Worcestershire, in 1932. A graduate of Keble College, Oxford, he taught for many years at the University of Leeds, then lectured at Cambridge as a Fellow of Emmanuel College. He is the author of six previous books of poetry and of *New and Collected Poems, 1952–1992*. His stage version of *Brand,* a dramatic poem by Ibsen, was commissioned by the National Theatre, London, and performed there in 1978. His critical writings have been published in two volumes, *The Lords of Limit* and *The Enemy's Country*, the latter based on his Clark Lectures delivered at Cambridge in 1986. Since 1988 he has been a member of The University Professors at Boston University.